MARTIAL SCIENCE

BIMONTHLY MAGAZINE OF MARTIAL ARTS   DECEMBER/2018 - Nº 27

KUBOTAN
SIFU JUSTIN CATALDI

COMBINATIONS OF SHINKAIDO RYU
HENRY BINERFA

PULAHAN MANDIRIGMA
FILIPINO MARTIAL ARTS
LAKAN MARC BEHIC

THE INDIANA JONES OF THE NINJUTSU WORLD – JAMES LEE
BY MASTER GUY EDWARD LARKE

Master Apolo Ladra
Baltimore, Maryland

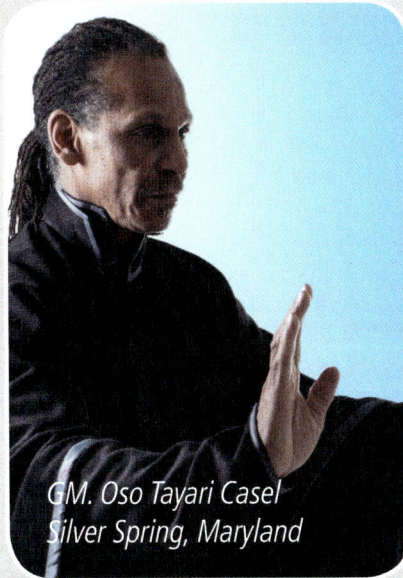
GM. Oso Tayari Casel
Silver Spring, Maryland

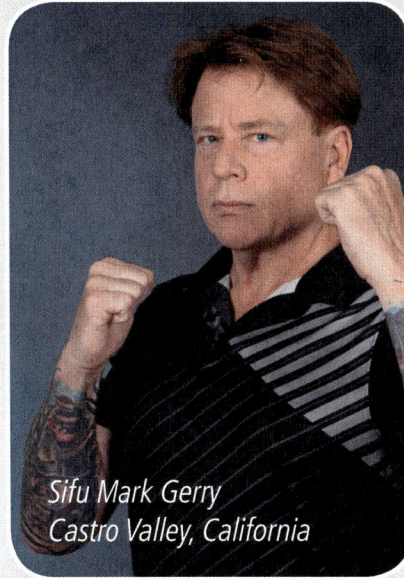
Sifu Mark Gerry
Castro Valley, California

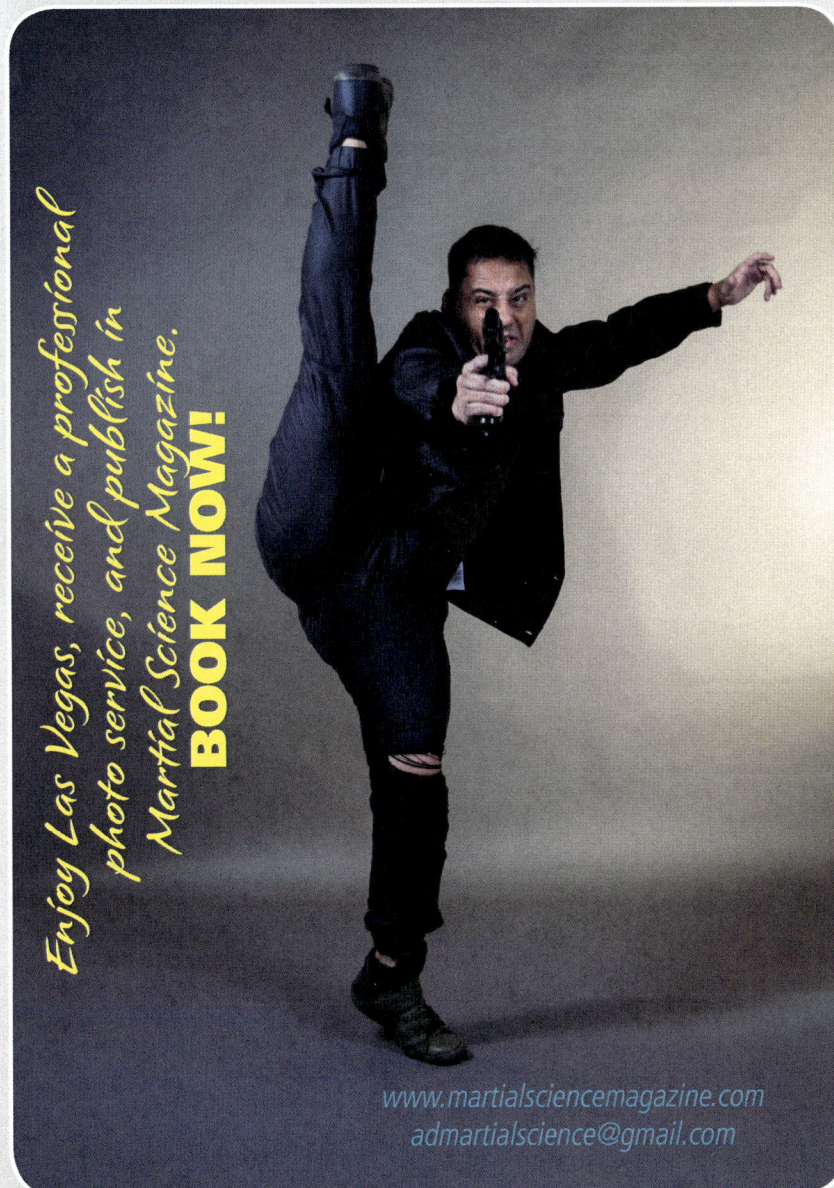
Soke Dave Johnson
Fresno, California

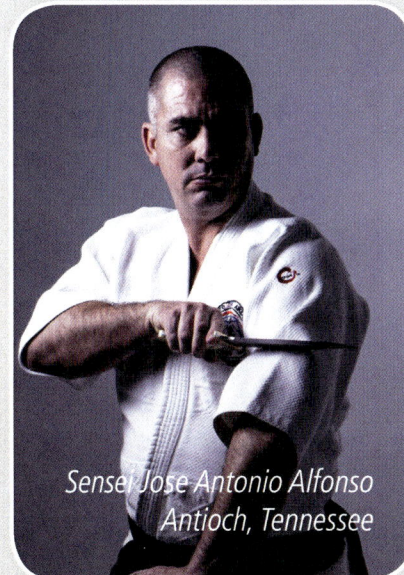

Enjoy Las Vegas, receive a professional photo service, and publish in Martial Science Magazine. **BOOK NOW!**

www.martialsciencemagazine.com
admartialscience@gmail.com

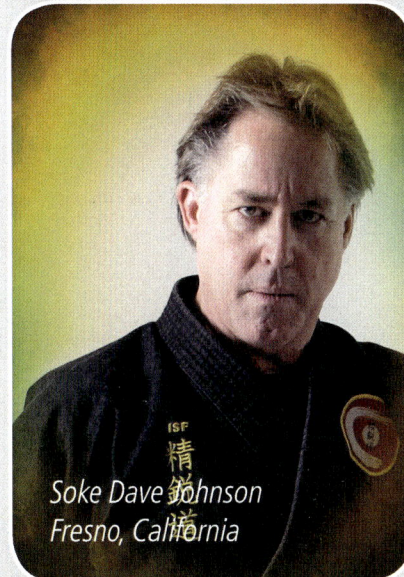
Sensei Jose Antonio Alfonso
Antioch, Tennessee

Contents

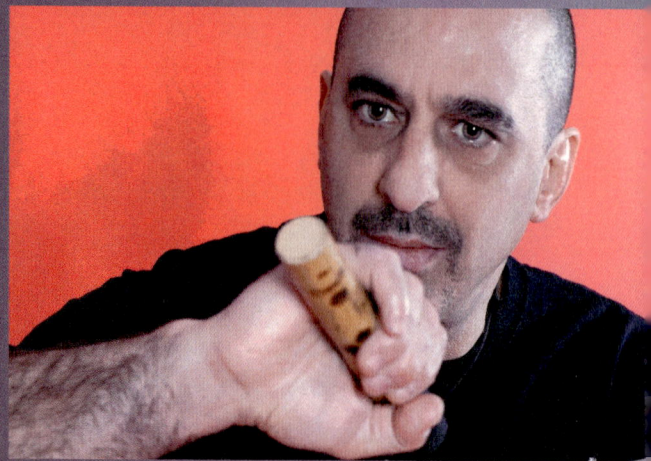

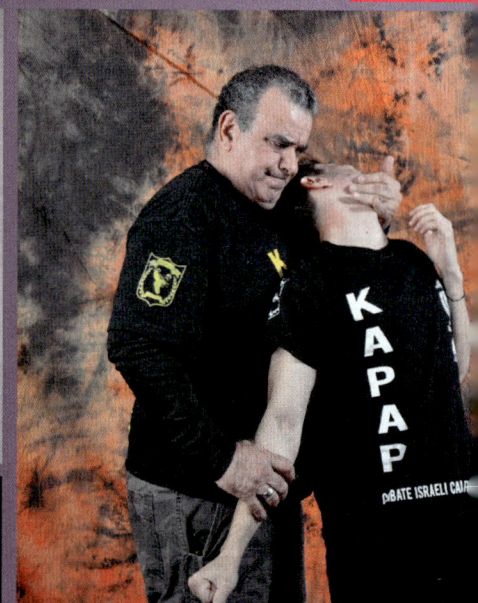

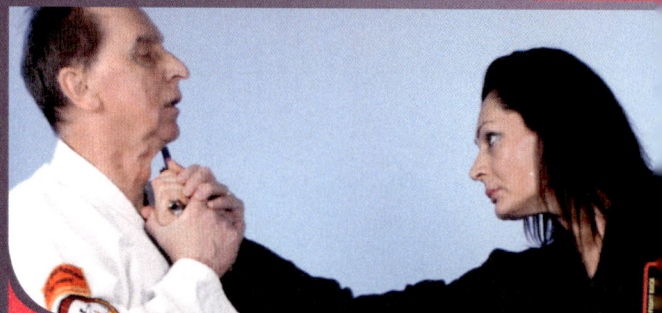

Martial Science
MAGAZINE
DECEMBER/2018 - N° 27

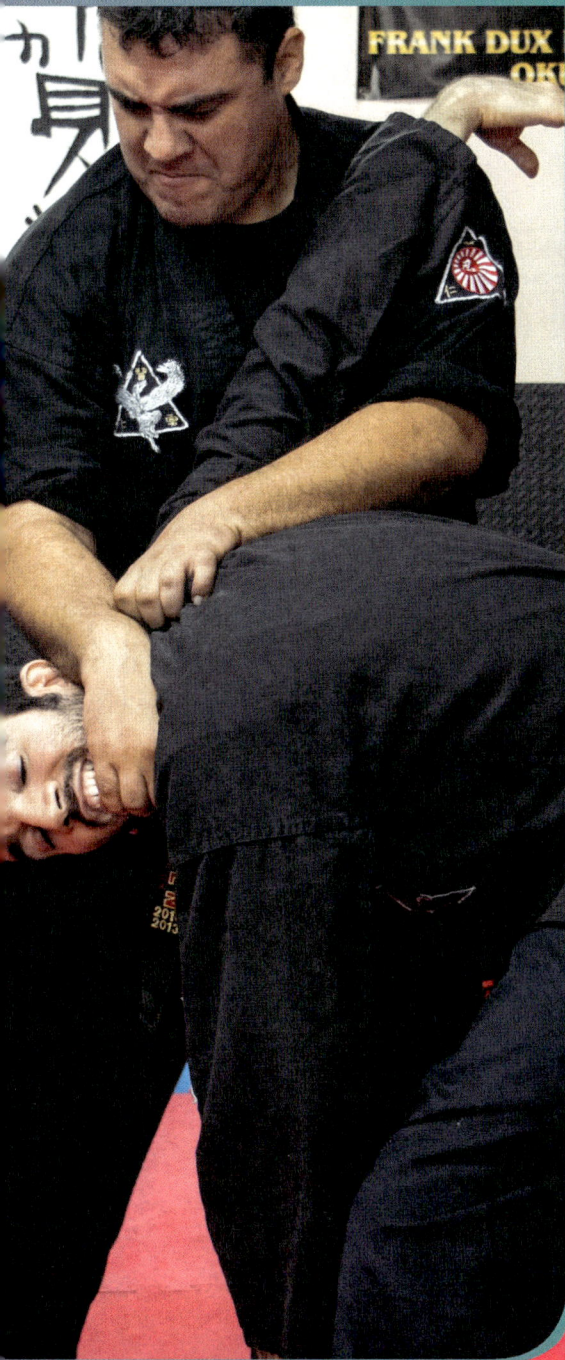

> *"The warrior learns of the spiritual realm by dwelling on the cutting edge of the sword, standing at the edge of the fire pit, venturing right up to the edge of starvation if necessary. Vibrant and intense living is the warrior's form of worship."*
> **-Stephen K. Hayes**

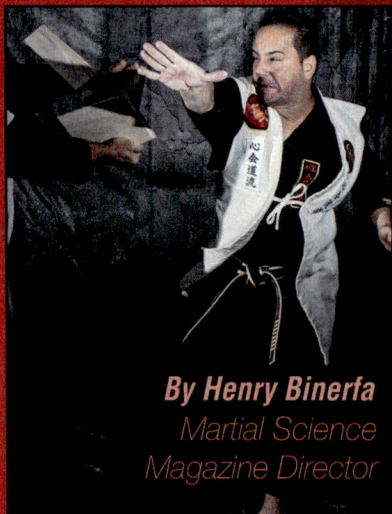

By Henry Binerfa
*Martial Science
Magazine Director*

"...Jita Kyoei - Based on mutual support, solidarity and helping seekers find the way to their own perfection..."

MARTIAL ARTS AND MODERN TIMES

EVERY SATURDAY I TRAIN AT THE DOJO OF THE NO KAGE RYU KENPO KARATE, FROM SENSEI JIMMY LOCKETT. SENSEI JIMMY IS A GREAT PERSON WITH A WIDE EXPERIENCE IN DIFFERENT MARTIAL ARTS. HIS DOJO HAS BECOME A MEETING POINT FOR SEVERAL EXPERTS IN DIFFERENT MARTIAL ARTS. EACH TRAINING IS NOT ONLY PHYSICAL BUT ALSO AN EXCHANGE OF QUESTIONS AND ANSWERS THAT ARISE INSTANTANEOUSLY AT ANY TIME OF TRAINING, WHICH ALWAYS TRY TO FIND A BETTER WAY TO TRAIN OR RESPOND TO A REAL SELF-DEFENSE SITUATION.

Recently we talked about the development of technology and how we could use it to attract new generations to the practice of martial arts. In the conversation we did not have the same criteria all, as almost always happens, but, although sometimes we walk in different ways the goal is the same.

I am making books, almost all my system has been in ink and paper. In the debate it was said that the new generations do not like books, that we are in the digital age. Young boys just want to open the phone and search for the videos on YouTube and learn from them. And this, honestly, made me think and investigate on the internet how other teachers used the net-

Martial Science Magazine, Volume 27, ISBN 9781795461030, is Published Bi-monthly, (February, April, June, August, October, and December) by Martial Science Publications LLC., Phone: (702)439-9071 Website: www.martialsciencemagazine.com - Email: admartialscience@gmail.com. All rights reserved.

works. Beyond the youtuber of martial arts and their blogs I also saw that there are online courses to learn martial arts. Today you can become a black belt even without leaving the house, and my astonishment went further when I saw that you could get the black belt in one year.

Everything I found was not negative. I can say that I saw some teachers with very good videos, with explanations and advice that serve as a guide for practitioners of any level.

Thanks to the internet, today with a few clicks we can have access to an infinity of information. In the case of martial arts, many see a video tutorial of martial arts and believe that because they see it two or three times they already master the techniques. There are also many who download many books, or have paper books on their shelves and believe that by having them there they dominate everything they contain. I tell them that they are collectors of martial information, sometimes a lot of theory and very little practice. All teaching to be fruitful must be lived

In the end I summarize that everything depends on Man. If man feels that strength, that real need, that urge to learn martial arts, he can learn it even when he sees the animals fighting, as did the ancestors of the past. In my country and the time in which I lived my youth, the information of the martial arts in printed media was very limited, and not to mention audio visual materials. If someone owned a magazine or a martial arts book, it was as if he had a great treasure.

I remember that person trained his content so conscientiously that he could surely go to a championship and possibly win with the techniques that he learned from that book or magazine. That is why I say that everything depends on the attitude of man.

I am particularly firmly rooted in the idea that the presence of the teacher is necessary and irreplaceable, I recognize that any medium used is good for the teaching-learning process. But there is nothing like the presence of a teacher who transmits the teachings from lip to ear. Technology has helped us to get very far, as far as the Moon itself, but there are places where we can only arrive in the same way that the saints and sages of the past arrived. There are no rockets that lead us to know ourselves, or teach us the depth of our spirit. At least so far for that trip we can only be taken by the hand of the Master.
Happy New Year!

Henry Binerfa | Publisher/CEO
Martial Science Publications, LLC

SPECIAL EDITION COLLECTIONS
Vol 1,2 And 3

746 pages and many images of the best of these three years published in Martial Science Magazine.

A GREAT DEAL

Buy Now

SINGLE ISSUE PRINT VERSION

Buy Now

PUBLISHER/EDITOR -IN-CHIEF
Henry Binerfa C.

CREATIVE DIRECTOR
Diosmel Acuña

COLUMNISTS
Master Guy Larke Edward
Sensei Jimmy Lockett

CONTRIBUTORS
GM. Pablo Rodarte
GM. Mark Shuey
James Wilson
Master Airr Phanthip
GM. Samuel Kwok
Sifu Bob Goméz
Sifu Justin Cataldi
Master Wong
Master Nar Babao
GM. Bernd Hoehle
GM. Dave Johnson
GM. Jeff Speakman

TRANSLATIONS
Yisel Viamontes
Daryanis Tamayo Fuente

心会道流

本部

HOMBU DOJO
SHINKAIDO RYU

For seminars or
representations,
write to:

internationalshinkaido@gmail.com
www.shinkaidoryu.org

Learn about:

Self-Defense Situations

Self-Defense Strategies

Techniques and Combinations

SENSEI HENRY BINERFA

Martial Science MAGAZINE
www.cienciamartial.com

NEWS

Visit of Sensei Henry Binerfa the Dojo of Dux Ryu in Puerto Rico

Photos By: Yisel Viamontes

ON OCTOBER 25, 1 VISITED PUERTO RICO. ON THE OCCASION OF MY TOUR OF SOUTH AMERICA FOR THE DISSEMINATION OF THE SHINKAIDO RYU. TO ENTER THE MARTIAL WORLD OF THE CITY OF SAN JUAN, 1 BEGAN TO SEARCH THE CITY ONLINE UNTIL 1 MET LUIS TORRES RIVERA WHO KINDLY GUIDED ME AND INTRODUCED ME TO THE DUX RYU SYSTEM IN PUERTO RICO LED BY SENSEI VÍCTOR ENRIQUE SUAREZ.

The Dux Ryu Ninjutsu is derived from the Koga Yamabushi Ryu school and popularized by Hanshi Frank W. Dux, and the film Bloodsport, starring Jean Claude Van Damme. Frank W. Dux was a student of Senzo "Tigre" Tanaka (1888 - 1975), a prominent member of the Kokuryukai, a Japanese intelligence officer and the first champion of the tournament known as Kumite.

Sensei Victor was very kind, even allowed me to show my techniques in his Dojo, and share with his more advanced students. All with a very good training not only in the technical, but also very respectful and with high martial values. The work of Sensei Victor is undoubtedly reflected in the behavior of his students. His work goes far beyond the walls of his Dojo as he teaches in different schools of the city special workshops on prevention and self-defense, motivational talks and his project

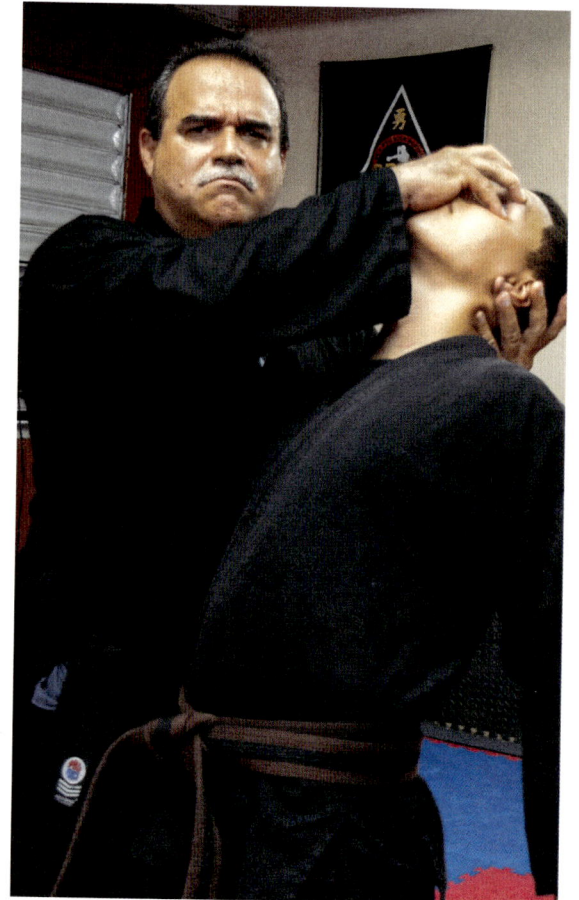

Pateando al Bully has been a good way to reinforce the educational values of the little ones, educating respect, courtesy, and teamwork.

My visit to Puerto Rico was a success, because I was able to make good friends, share my experience in martial arts with good people and also enjoy the beaches and the excellent Food of Isla del Encanto.

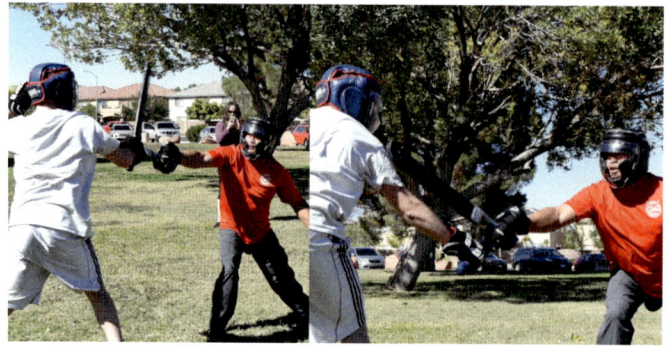

First Vegas Fight Lab 2018 Hosted by Creative Warrior Academy

CREATIVE WARRIOR ACADEMY WAS HONORED TO HOST THE FIRST VEGAS FIGHT LAB EVER ON OCTOBER 14 , 2018 . ALL FMA SPARRING GEAR WAS SUPPLIED BY BUNAL BRAND FMA GEAR . THE EVENT WAS HELD AT WAYNE BUNKER FAMILY PARK , WHICH IS A BEAUTIFUL LITTLE PARK IN NORTH LAS VEGAS

This gathering was an effort to create a community where Vegas Filipino Martial Arts Schools could meet in a neutral and friendly manner, and share friendship and wisdoms with one another . The event was very successful as we were able to bring together 7 local vegas schools, 1 school from Phoenix Arizona, and 2 schools in california . Las Vegas schools consisted of ; myself and my student Casey DeChant from Creative Warrior Academy Kali/JKD , Guro Manny Valladares and his students Anthony Balisacan and Marco Parayno from JKD Unlimited , Richard Palacios from Las Vegas Kung Fu Academy , Roy Corpus and Eric Lopez from Largusa Kali, Guro TJ Cuenca from Superhero Foundry , Sensei Henry Binerfa from Shinkaido Ryu Las Vegas and GM Marc Behic of Pulahan Mandirigma Las Vegas. Traveling from LA we had Bunal Brand founder and Doce Pares Master Steve Del Castillo , and from San Diego my close personal friends and most honored FMA ambassadors GM Zena Babao and Master Nar Babao of Babao Arnis systems. Finally we had Sensei Curt Jablin , FMA fighter and Instructor of Doce Pares.

As everyone began to show up we all took time to get to know one another, and enjoy some great conversation . Since this event was not a tournamen, it was a very relaxed and friendly gathering. After awhile we all participated in light sparring of different kinds, including padded knife sparring, sword sparring, and stick sparring, finishing off with two on one sparring! We used light protection such as lacrosse gloves , padded weapons and head protection which covered the face . Everyone had a great time, got to try out the Bunal sparring equipment, and enjoy the park, while meeting new friends. I had the great honor of sparring with some very high level Masters and learning some great things that

will enhance my martial arts skills and interpretations. We spent several hours, trading training drills and ideas, and getting a great workout!

Afterwards we all worked up a hearty appetite, so we headed over to the Olive Garden to sit together and enjoy some delicious pasta and italian margaritas! It has become somewhat of a tradition to bring Auntie Zena and Master Nar to eat at this restaurant for my wife and I, so we figured why don't we just all go eat together ! There's nothing better than sharing great food with great people, and the Babaos are the best!

Hopefully this will be the beginning of a com-munity that appreciates and practices Filipino Martial Arts in Las Vegas for years to come. Since this gathering we have met again twice, once again at the park and then at JKD unlimited headquarters , where we worked some knife grappling technique! It was truly fabulous to meet again to train and continue to bond as a martial arts family. As a group we decided on the name Las Vegas FMA Groups, and we are welcoming any FMA groups in our city to join us anytime. Our next meeting will be at Creative Warrior Academy of Las Vegas, on November 18th and this time its stick sparring with a potluck at the end! Nothing brings people together faster than food , and we will be quite hungry from some great training and sparring!

Through the open minded and friendly manner behind our meetings we hope to promote Filipino Martial Arts as a whole, and educate the public in our areas of the potential and benefits of FMA, not only as a method of self defense, but also a method of growth and change in everyday life. Hope to see all of you at our next vegas fight lab ! Thank you, Live Well and Train Hard! Sifu/Guro Justin Cataldi, senior Instructor at Creative Warrior Academy of Las Vegas.

Written by Sifu Justin Cataldi
Photography and editing by Sensei Henry Binerfa

The Munich Hall of Honours
2019@munichhalloffame.com

Dear Martial Arts Family!

The 12th Edition of Europe`s finest Martial Arts Event of its kind will again be setting new trends in all areas. Beeing held in Munich, Bavaria, one of the most favorite spots in the world, as the promoter I was very happy to find two years ago one of the oldest, very unique and typical venue's in this popular bavarian capitol, the HOFBRÄU KELLER am Wiener Platz.
From 1896 to 1988 it was the Brewery for the famous Hofbräu Beer and already early the beer garden on top of the beer stocks became popular with Munich citizens. It is not the typical tourist place like the HOFBRÄU HAUS in downtown, but a history-charged place with fantastic food and typical bavarian atmosphere and all attendees of the event love it. You can easy reach with public transportation which is very convinient for our large comunity of international quest.

Therefore it will be the venue for the 2019 Event again.
There is a few wellknown Hotel within 1-2 km and good connections. Courtyard by Marriot, Motel One, Hilton Hotel, Holiday Inn and more, some within walking distance.“

Meet our quest and celebrities from all over the world

Many celebrities, legends, grandmasters and masters with their students have confirmed their attendance like The Queen of Martial Arts Movies, Cynthia Rothrock, 11times Pro Boxing World Champion Daisy „The Lady“ Lang, German Hollywood Star Matthias Hues, Wing Chun Legend Samuel Kwok, and Karen Trolan Martial Artist, Speaker and Author of „I CAN STILL DO IT!“

The Unstoppable Spirit of a Plane Crash Survivor, Canadian Actor and Olympic Champion Sunny Singh, european Legends and Grandmasters like GM Juerg Ziegler, CH Soke Heinz Köhnen, GER Hanshi Herbert E. Forster, CH Austrain Olympic Diving Champion and Karate GM Erhard Kellner, GM Perry Zmugg, Wushu Legend Sifu Serge Seguin, from UK Olympic Champion and Actor Silvio Simac, 11times Worldchampion Extreme Martial Arts Master Emma Elmes and for the first time GM Gary Wasniewski, Kickbox Word and European Champions Bernie Willems und Ferdinand Mack, Actress and Filmproducer Ugyen Choden from Buthan, and many many more.

Many more will be there but have not been confirmed yet.

There will be many champions from martial arts, fitness and health at this most recognized event in Europe, stars and starlets from the martial arts and action movies, stuntman and stuntwoman, local and worldrenown and of course all the Black Belts, Instructors and Students which are nominated by their Grandmasters and Masters for their achievements in the martial arts.

The Best and most prestegiouse event in Europe since 12 years

„During the day on saturday, 30 of the best instructors and experts in their field will have again the chance to present their style to the large crowd in a 45 Min short clinic.

The celebrities an selected Persons of interest will be able to present their books, DVD`s or good to the audience in a small trade show.

The „strong man/woman" Contest is organised and supervised again by multiple Weightlifting Word Champion Benno Stangl and his Team, where the winners in 4 categories will be awarded with a trophy during the evening ballot.

Of course there will be spectacular shows at the evening awards banquett and everyone will

love the large buffet with typical bavarian and international kitchen ."

The traditional Welcome Party will be on Friday, starting at 6 p.m. in a typical bavarian venue and will be another life time experience for those who attend.

Off course the whole event will be covered by Martial Science Magazine and many other media, featured on Social media and local media. If you want to be part of this most prestigeouse event, don't hesitate to book as soon as possible, since space is, as always, very limited to only those who decide fast. If want to nominate a deserved Martial Artists dont hesitate to write us for more information:

2019@munichhalloffame.com

THE INDIANA JONES OF THE NINJUTSU WORLD

By Master Guy Edward Larke

It is hard to be an individual. It is harder to do it a conservative environment. Now try to be a leader of many on top of that. For young readers that may not seem like a big deal but for us more "seasoned" veterans it was a challenging reality. The ideals of the Chinese classic, Outlaws of the Water Margin are wonderful, but those characters too were social pariah.

Growing up in small towns in Canada and even a few small cities in Korea, I knew the feelings of alienation for being different. Fortunately, through my writing I learned there is no need to be an island. One of those bridges came from a good friend, Grandmaster AVS Bathi of Kuala Lumpur. He introduced me to a very eclectic group of martial artists who bond regardless of race, art, or religion. The group was called the Malaysian Wen Wu Martial Arts Association. The head of it being a long haired Ninjutsu instructor who was one-part warrior, one-part philosopher, and one part rebel who looked like he belonged in the USA or Canada rather than Malaysia.

What kind of person would follow the path he had interested me both as a writer and as a martial artist. Here are a few of the answers...

James, or Lee Peek-Kuan, born on March 11th, 1965 in Perak State in Malaysia. He grew up with his parents and two younger brothers. It was a very conservative upbringing for the boys.

There was no real martial arts information at the time. Most of what was available was manhua (Chinese comic books) and Shaw Brothers films. James couldn't afford such luxuries so he just listened to his friends' retelling of the adventures and let his imagination run wild. Like myself on the other side of the world, he fantasized about heroes overcoming injustice despite overwhelming odds. This escapism helped him deal with the circumstances he grew up in as a young boy.

When his family moved to the town of Taiping he secretly tried Tae Kwon Do and Shaolin Pai (a Hokkien style from Singapore). Eventually his parents discovered and allowed him to continue. As he never really had any preconceptions both arts were a great experience for him. Of course because he was Chinese he favoured the Chinese art a bit more. Eventually he couldn't afford both so he chose the Chinese art. Already at that point he secretly experimented with mixing the two.

That started an interest or rather a thirst for new things. While doing Shaolin Pai in the Taiping Hokkien Association, he also dabbled in Silat Kampung with a little smattering of Thai Boxing. He was forced to relocate in order to attend TAR College for three years. As he was without a master again he got the opportunity to study Village Style

THE INDIANA JONES OF THE
NINJUTSU WORLD

Hung Gar. He managed to exchange some skills and patterns with some new friends, one of whom passed on two Chinese Vagabond patterns to me.

After graduation his job took him far South to the city of Johor Baru where he took up ITF Taekwon-Do. It was during that period that something happened that changed his life irrevocably.

He happened upon an article by Mahaguru Azlan Ghanie about a gentleman who claimed to be a Bujinkan (a style of

Ninjutsu) master. He met and trained with him. He joined with what turned out to be a pseudo Ninjutsu group whose founder claimed he was from the Bujinkan but did not offer any proof despite James' inquiries. Formally, he only trained under him for about four or five months before returning to Kuala Lumpur. He also helped him to register a martial art association. On his own, hedeveloped a free style syllabus while was very much influenced by Robert Bussey despite the displeasure of the pseudo Ninjutsu founder who claimed it wasn't true Ninjutsu. Yet, he could not explained what true Ninjutsu is either. Frustrated, James left him the association he set up for him after two years. By then, Lee knew he wasn't as claimed. The young instructor abandoned what he developed and concentrated on Soke's tapes, his books and whatever material he can lay his hands on. He wanted to know what the Bujinkan was all about. During that period he became exposed to international magazines, books,

and videos. James became very inspired by Robert Bussey of Warrior International. Bussey was famous for mixing Ninjutsu with kickboxing, Hapkido, flashy kicks and so on. With this new philosophy he continued on teaching with his mentor and taught a similar syllabus to Bussey.

After a few years the two parted ways and went their own ways. He began searching for a real Bujinkan link and put the word out everywhere. Later he

began adding to their collective knowledge. He trained James and his group for 2 years before he moved to Japan. Boesen awarded him his 2nd Dan after training his protégé. He also went to Japan to get Lee's Japanese certificate from the headmaster, Dr. Masaaki Hatsumi.

During James' many readings he discovered many instructors simply visited Japan short time, practiced at home and returned at a later date to refine and move onward. Technology changed how people could learn. He began to do the same.

THE INDIANA JONES OF THE
NINJUTSU WORLD

received a call from Master William Boesen (a retired Danish military officer living and working in Malaysia and Bujinkan expert). He reached out to James in need of a good training partner.

After meeting Boesen was surprised how much James' students actually knew and

While teaching Bujinkan Ninjutsu, he met a school teacher whose father used to teach Kung Fu in the 1960s. It came from three wandering Hakka people. His father stopped teaching and retired in the 1970s. Old age diminished his memories until what he used to teach became lost. The teacher who became his student was doing other arts like Tae Kwon Do, etc. and had no interest in what his father used to teach. Lee managed to persuade this student to show him what he could remember of what was taught to him during his teenage years. While a

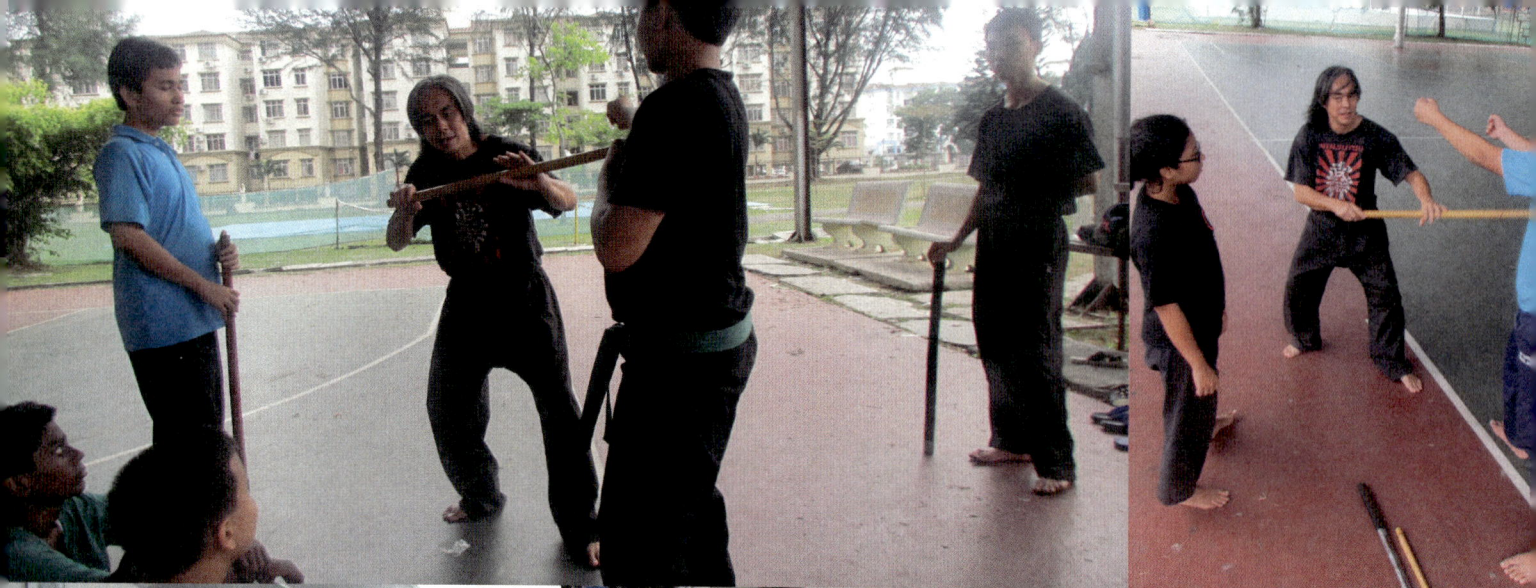

lot was lost, Lee managed to salvage, expand and improve on whatever was left. Combining this with the earlier Vagabond patterns and others which he picked up and exchanged with others, a complete Malaysian Vagabond System materialized with emphasis on the Tiger.

Around this time e noticed many other local arts were dying. He even looked at his own background and realized in certain arts he was part of the last generation. His own grandmaster in the Bujinkan served as a good example to what these arts needed to do. They needed to open their doors to the world.

So he created the Malaysian Wen Wu Martial Arts Association and reached out to like-minded individuals. The original group consisted of:

1) Ben Tan (Yip Kin Wing Chun)
2) DL Goh (Hung Gar)
3) Himself
4) Sifu Yap Boh Heong, Sifu Chong Chin Kean (Chee Kim Tong 5 Ancestors Fist)
5) Brendan Lanza (Silat Chimande)
6) Fong Ying Nam (WTF Tae Kwon Do, Sanda)
7) Teh Kok Leong (Pekiti Tersia, 5 Ancestors Kung Fu, various Chinese arts)
8) Sifu Sim Kam Fatt (Yip Man Wing Chun)
9) Sifu Lai Ho Lin (Lion Dance)
10) Lim Chee Hong (Choy Lay Futt Kung Fu)

Currently he is in the process of writing a book on Malaysian Vagabond / Wanderer Tiger Fist. After he plans to write a few more, with the first few ones on the arts which are on the verge of extinction and which can't be found in China. Sensei Lee is still searching for whatever can be salvaged in the Malaysian landscape.

CONTACT INFORMATION:

Facebook
– Malaysian Wenwu Martial Arts Association
- Bujinkan Hachiman Dojo

Home Page:
www.malaysiabujinkan.com

MASTER GUY EDWARD LARKE has been involved in the martial arts and interested in Asian culture for most of his life. It brought him to Korea 18 years ago where he teaches various disciplines and writes for several magazines. He is also the Associate Editor for Seni Beladiri. Master Larke visits Malaysia regularly to teach seminars on Korean martial arts. He can be found on Facebook or at kisdaomuye@gmail.com.

AFFILIATION PROGRAM MEMBERSHIP

The membership program of Martial science Magzine was created as an option for owners of schools, organizations, institutions, associations or vendors of products related to the sport and martial arts and who need to publish 2 or more publications in the year or marketing campaigns of long duration.

Recommended 100% to promote events, tournaments and seminars, to increase the number of students in your school, show your product to thousands of people, promote equipment for sports training or martial arts, supplements vitamin, in short all the related to the martial arts industry and sport.

Join Us!

BRONZE MEMBERSHIP.

- You can publish in 2 issues of Martial Science Magazine

- You can publish in only one language

- You can participate in events organized by Martial Science Magazine (national or international) with a discount of 10% of the regular price.

- You can have a table of sales in our events with a 10% discount off regular price.

- Ad in all the social networks of Martial Science Magazine of an occasional way

SILVER MEMBERSHIP.

- You can publish in 3 issues of Martial Science Magazine

- You can publish in only one language

- You can participate in events organized by Martial Science Magazine (national or international) with a discount of 20% of the regular price.

- You can have a table of sales in our events with a 20% discount off regular price.

- Ad in all the social networks of Martial Science Magazine of an occasional way

- A photo session Studio or out doors at a discount of 20% of the regular price. (disk + 10 printed photo)

GOLD MEMBERSHIP.

- You can publish in 6 issues of Martial Science Magazine

- You can publish in two language (english and spanish)

- You can participate in events organized by Martial Science Magazine (national or international) with a discount of 30% of the regular price.

- You can have a table of sales in our events with a 30% discount off regular price.

- Ad in our official website and in all the social networks of Martial Science Magazine for a year

- A photo session Studio or out doors at a discount of 30% of the regular price. (disk + 14 printed photo)

- Unique and preferential price of the print version of Martial Science Magazine

- Free publication in special issues of the Martial Science Magazine

Email:
martialscience@gmail.com
www.martialsciencemagazine.com

FILIPINO MARTIAL ARTS
PULAHAN MANDIRIGMA
LAKAN MARC BEHIC
Photos By: Henry Binerfa

How old were you when you started martial arts?

I started Martial Arts when I was 5 years old in 1967, San Francisco under professor Greg Lontayo. Later we moved to Hawaii 1971. I trained with Sifu Kimo Wong Kung Fu and Wing Chun Do. Then in 1982-2017 trained with Master Bernard Nunies "Mana" Hawaiian Kenpo/Filipino Kali/Escrima. Also, at the same time taught trained with Grandmaster George Beleno Hawaii Budo/Lima Lama Lua. Trained Hardcore Street/Kali Kickboxing with Master Mike "Dogzilla" Tibbitts of Hawaii Dog Brothers for several years. I still teaching to this day with my brother Grandmaster Joe Behic. We both are also US Veterans and incorporate our military self-defense skills / hand to hand combat skills infused with our art. We have been training and teaching in martial arts 51 years.

Can you tell us about your family lineage?

My family lineage goes all the way back to 1870. My Great grandfather Felipe Bejic and brother Rufo Bejic were Pulahan Rebels Royal Escrimador Leaders/Generals. They were from Davao Mindinao/Phillipines. In 1890 went to fight in Cebu to fight other warring (Moro) tribes and Spanish soldiers. They had a bounty on their heads for killing hundreds of the enemy soldiers. They fought in mountains of Pinagumahan, Cebu "Snake Mountains" They Had a spiritual warrior power called "Anting Anting" they were hard to kill because of this gift (spiritual power) to protect the family.

My great grandfather (Son) Severeno escape on a boat in 1907 to Hawaii to work in sugar cane fields in Hawaii. They are called "Secadas" at the docks He changed our last name to Behic. Many of our family members changed their last name in phillipines and Hawaii so the would not be detected from bounty put on our family Warrior/Escrimadors Pulahan Mandirigma Rebels. Changed their names to this day in these variations (Bejec, Bejik, Bejic, Behic) are some of the know changes of our name to protect family. We are all related. They were siblings. On

"THEY HAD A BOUNTY ON THEIR HEADS FOR KILLING HUNDREDS OF THE ENEMY SOLDIERS. THEY FOUGHT IN MOUNTAINS OF PINAGUMAHAN, CEBU "SNAKE MOUNTAINS" THEY HAD A SPIRITUAL WARRIOR POWER CALLED "ANTING ANTING" THEY WERE HARD TO KILL BECAUSE OF THIS GIFT (SPIRITUAL POWER) TO PROTECT THE FAMILY"

We also incorporate pressure points/bone manipulation. I incorporate not only the physical aspect but Mental and Spirituasl Warrior.

the big Island of Hawaii my great grandfathers (Son) Severeno Magalso Behic worked in Sugar Cane fields as "Secada" and later moved to main island Oahu where here workerd in sugar cane fields. He started a Tagalo knife gang to protect the filipino workers from harm syndicate protection "Siniate". Later he passed away in 1950's his son was my dad Severeno Malgalso Behic. From Ewa Hawaiimy dad went in the military to join the US Army in Vietnam. He did 3 tours of service in Vietnam/Cambodia. Retired honorably after 25 years' service in US military and about 20 years civil service. All of my family members also joined US Army. Military too and we are all veterans/military soldiers. We are Pure warrior Vegas. pre- Royal Escrimador Bloodline Warriors "Mandirigma". Our bloodline runs from 1870 Mindinao/Cebu 2018 Hawaii/Las Pulahan (Escrimador Rebels/Mandirigma). That how we served our name "Pulahan Mandirigma Dojos/Legions". Our system is called the "Behic System": Dance of the Mandirigma. I am founder of Pulahan Mandirigma Dojos. My Co-Founder is Grandmaster Joe Behic/Co-Founder and wife Maria Behic (advisor), Sgt of Arms/ GM. Larry Ordonio/Houston, Texas. We have many affiliated Dojos that are part of our Pulahan Mandirigma Legions from Hawaii/ Team USA Hawaii GSBA/Las Vegas/Texas/Washington/New York/ Germany. We are unpredictable and unorthodox fighters. We have the deep roots and traditions but learn to adapt and flow around and through our opponents. Perpetuate our roots and our ancestors and arts will never die as long as we keep our traditions in our heart "Corazon" and Spirit and Soul! The rest is blood, sweat and tears.

What martial arts do you teach?

I teach Kali/escrima with Hawaiian Kenpo/Lima Lama Lua/Karate/ Aikido/KickBoxing, all mixed into one Pulahan Mandirigma (Warrior) Behic Systems. We also incorporate pressure points/bone manipulation. I incorporate not only the physical aspect but Mental and Spirituasl Warrior. Using Yin Yang forces. Hard is the physical aspect and soft is healing/massage (Hilot) and spiritual energy the highest level of filipino martial arts all combined into one.

"Walk the Walk of a warrior Mandirigma not talk the talk"

Give respect! You will get the same in return. Honor your roots!

Peace, love of the Martial Arts, hard training! Will always. Preserve our ways! Many Respect and Blessings

PULAHAN MANDIRIGMA
LAKAN MARC BEHIC

BEHIC SYSTEM
FOR STICK & KNIFE

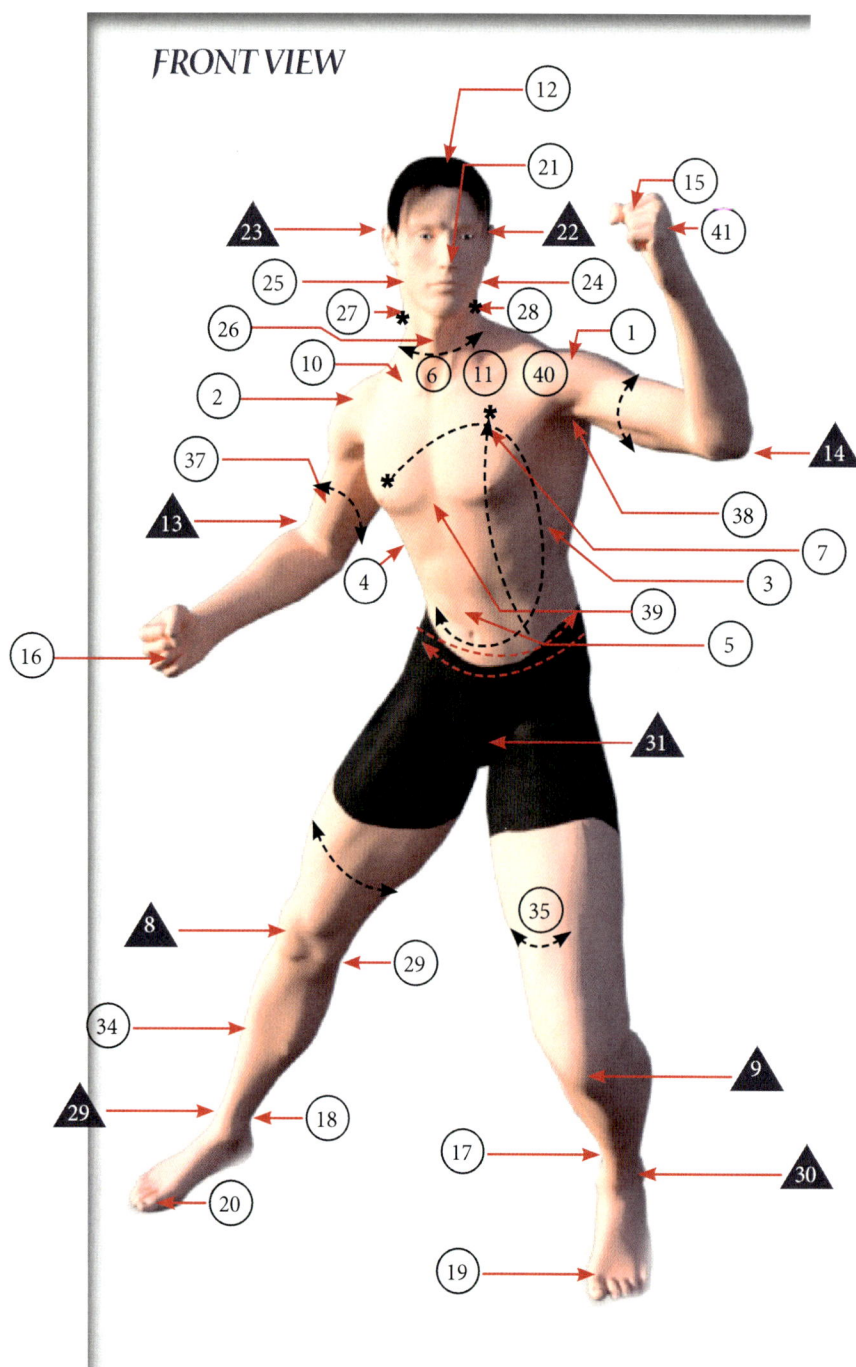

FRONT VIEW

1. Right Shoulder
2. Left Shoulder
3. Right Rib
4. Lef Rib
5. Stomach
6. Throat
7. Heart
8. Right Knee
9. Left Knee
10. Right Collarbone
11. Left Collarbone
12. Head
13. Right Elbow
14. Left Elbow
15. Left Fingers
16. Right Fingers
17. Left Ankle
18. Right Ankle
19. Left Toes
20. Right Toes
21. Nose
22. Left Ear
23. Right Ear
24. Left Jawbone
25. Right Jawbone
26. Cut off Neck
27. Rt. Knee (lift to face)
28. Lft. Knee (lift to face)
29. Right Ankle w/ foot brace/break
30. Left Ankle w/foot brace/break
31. Groin
32. Stick Behind knees
33. Follow up 1 and 2
34. Shins
35. Inside the Thighs
36. Floating Ribs
37. Median Nerve

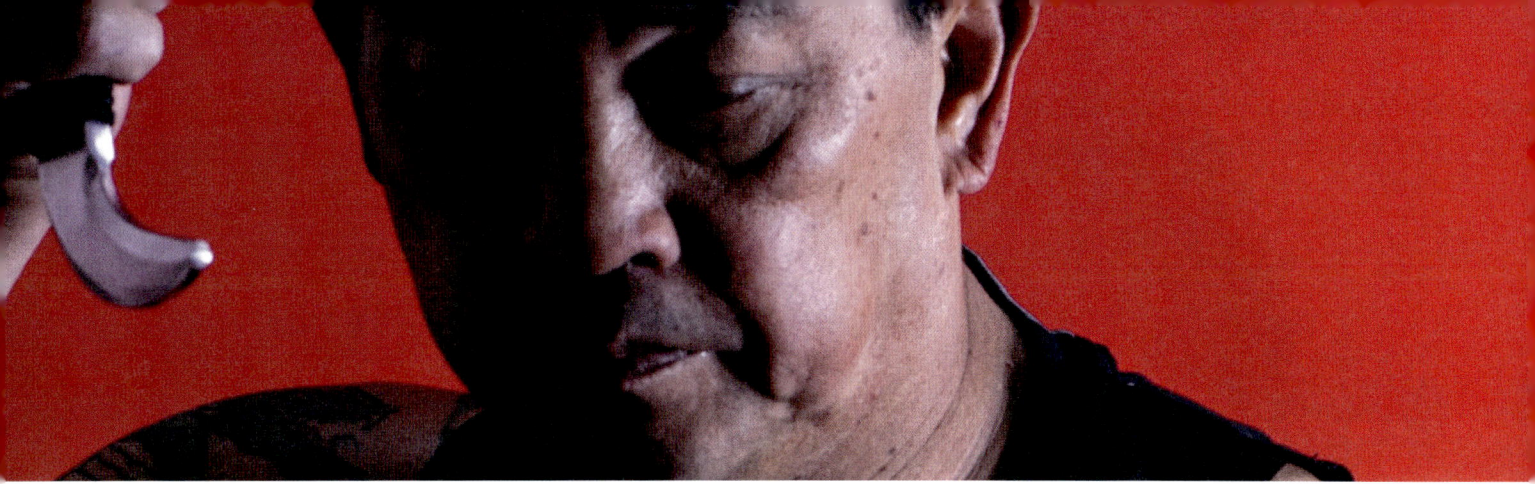

BACK VIEW

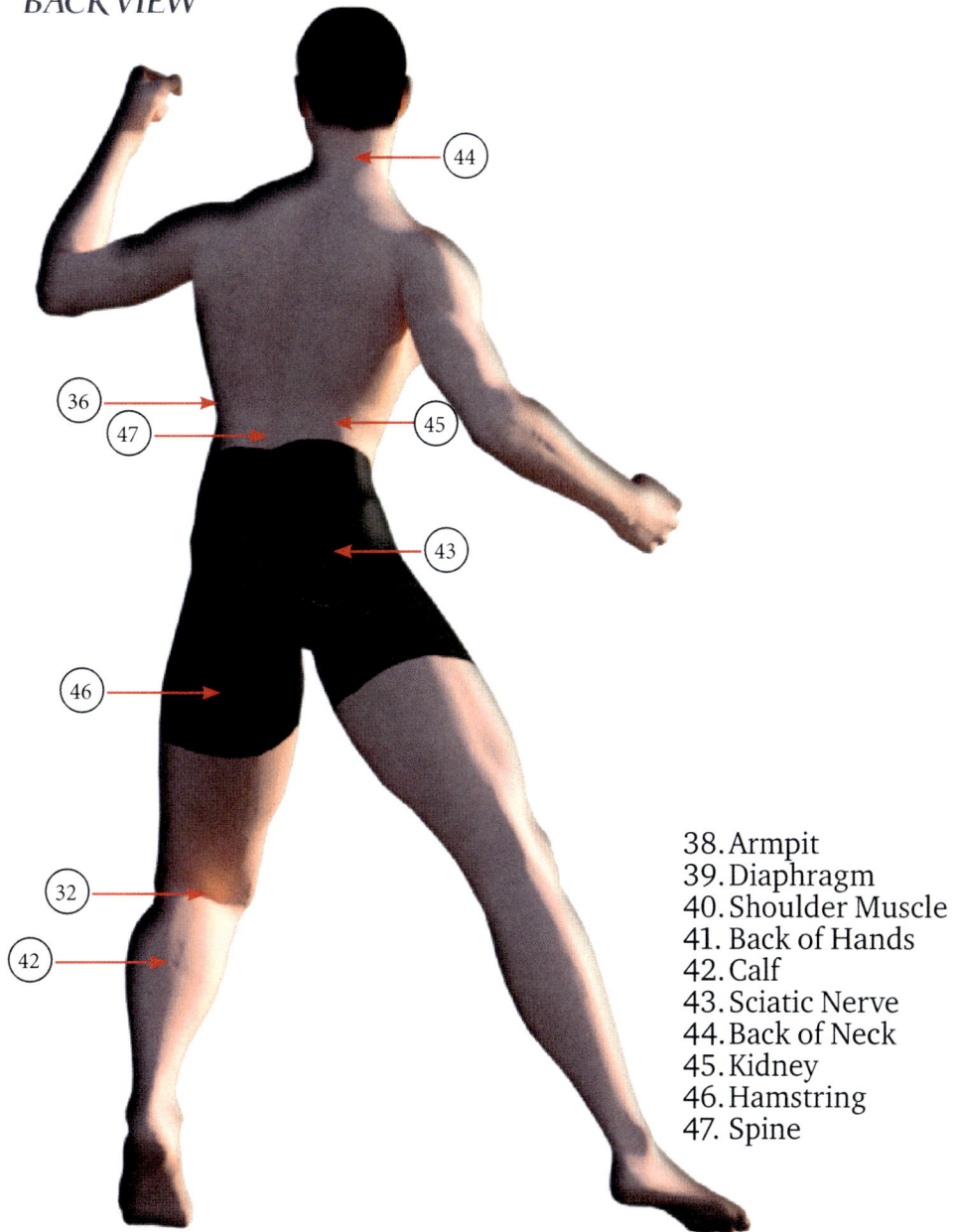

38. Armpit
39. Diaphragm
40. Shoulder Muscle
41. Back of Hands
42. Calf
43. Sciatic Nerve
44. Back of Neck
45. Kidney
46. Hamstring
47. Spine

FILIPINO MARTIAL ARTS
PULAHAN MANDIRIGMA
LAKAN MARC BEHIC

1

2

3

4

5

Marcbehic@gmail.com

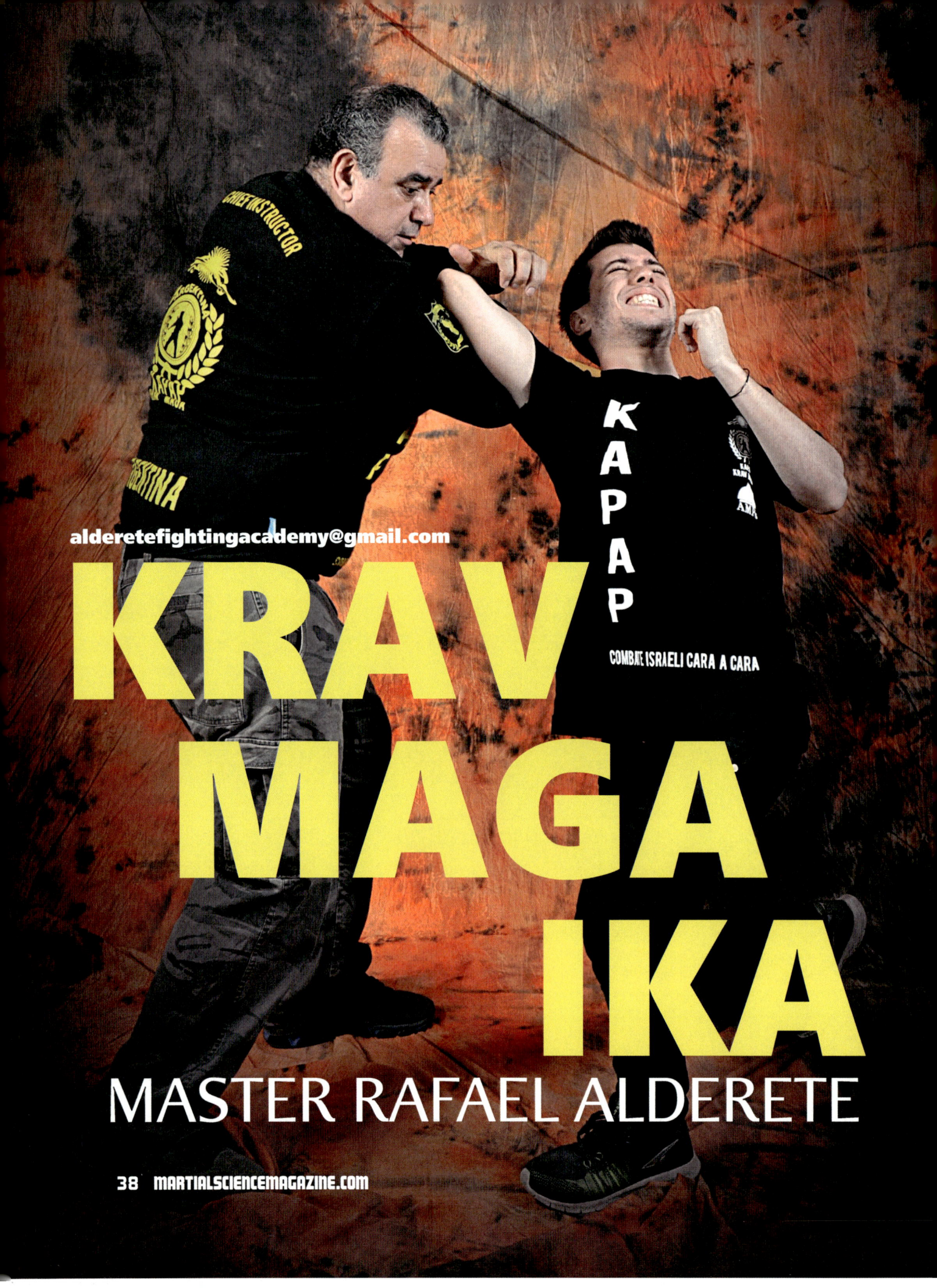

alderetefightingacademy@gmail.com

KRAV MAGA IKA

MASTER RAFAEL ALDERETE

MASTER RAFAEL ALDERETE

Taekwondo 7th Dan - Hapkido 6th Dan Kapap/Krav Maga I.K.A President Oficial Representative for ARGENTINA Level "C" Intructor +54 9 341-3937659 (whatsapp)

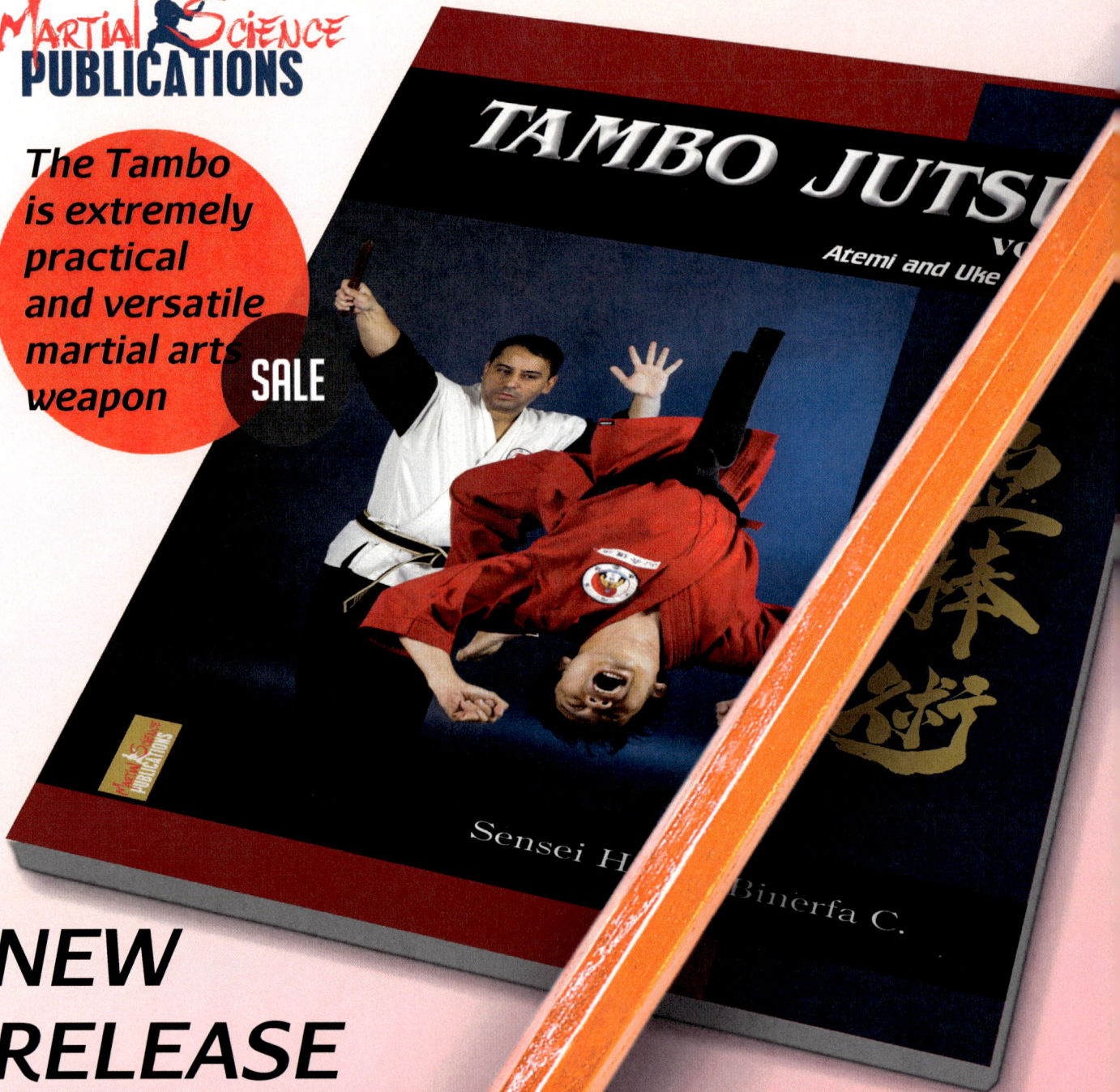

KUBOTAN

By: Sifu Justin Cataldi

Photos By: Henry Binerfa

The Kubotan was created by Takayuki Kubota in its full key form and as we know it today, among the weapons that preceded it we found the yawara and many more back in time a religious artifact called Vajra or Dorge that the Buddhist Monks carried with them as part of of his usual religious practice. The influence of Buddhism on the samurai caste gave rise to the later development of Yawara techniques, Tenssen Jutsu (fan technique) and Tanto Jutsu (knife techniques).

The martial arts Philippines adopted the Kubotan or Yawara probably after the Second World War and they called it Dulo Dulo. Despite being an adopted weapon of the Japanese fighting systems, the Filipinos provided a very different way of using it, making multiple movements and fluids of very fast attacks and included in their practice various exercises to develop sensitivity.

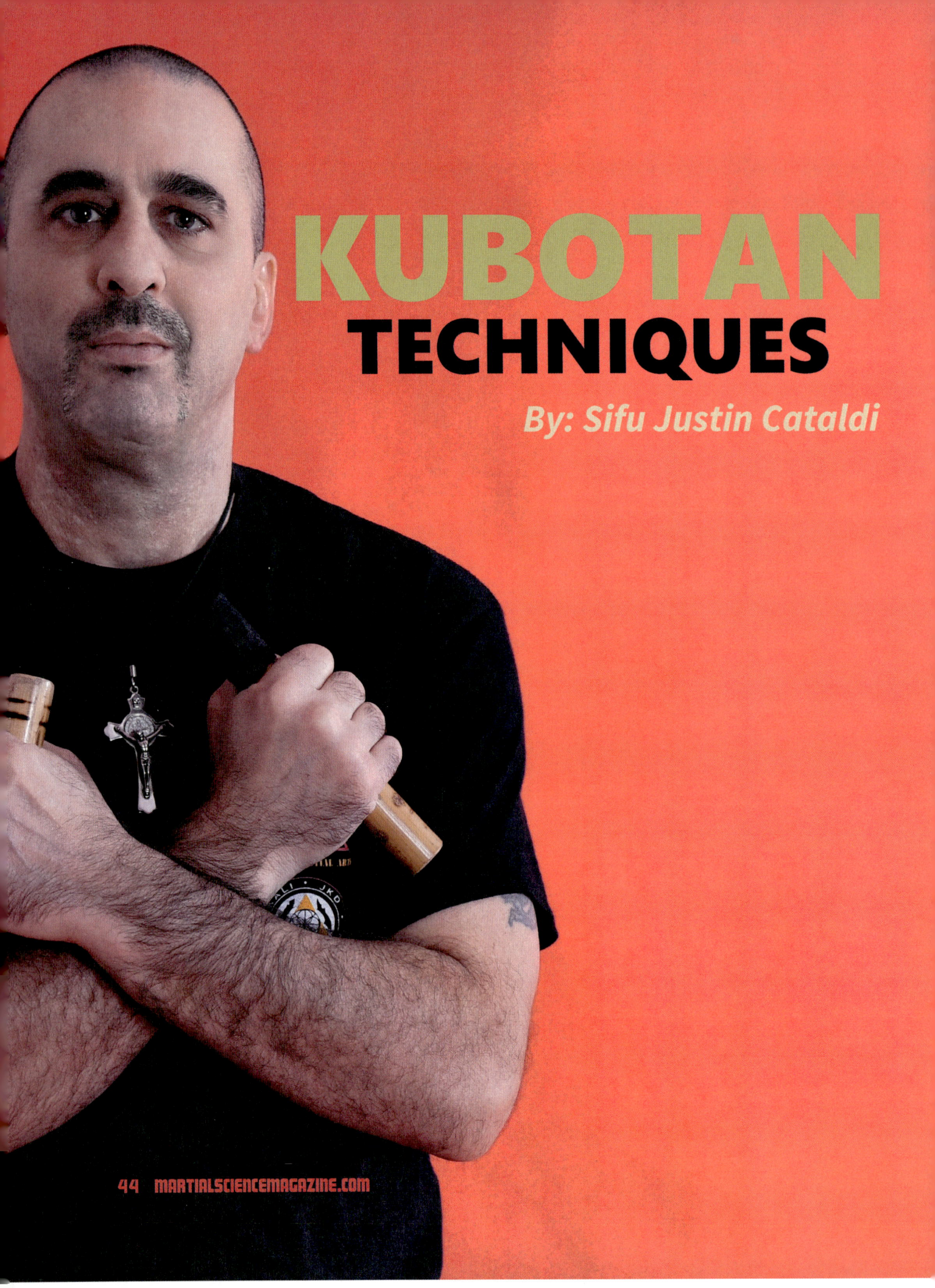

KUBOTAN
TECHNIQUES

By: Sifu Justin Cataldi

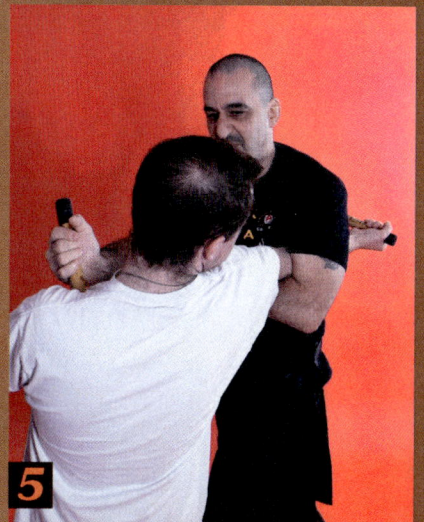

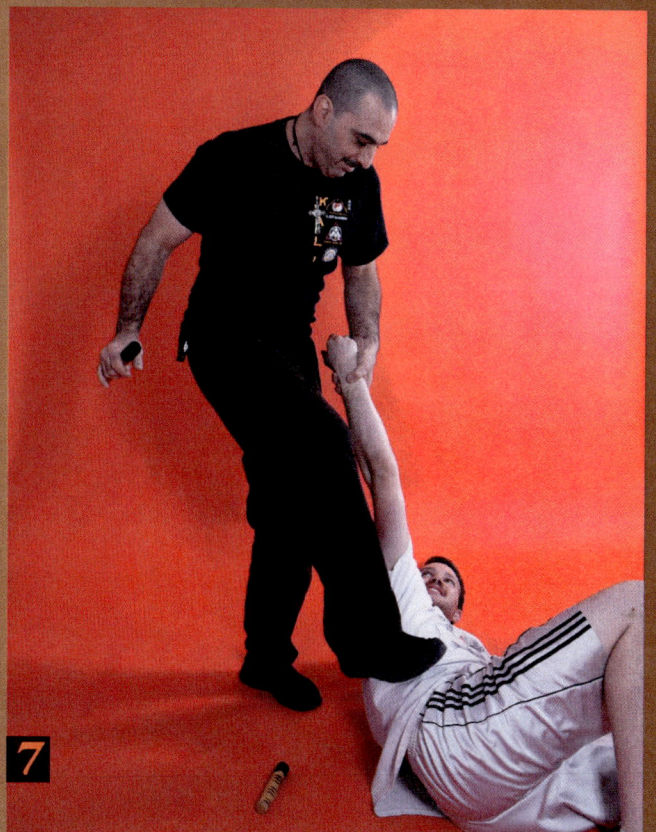

KUBOTAN
TECHNIQUES

1

2

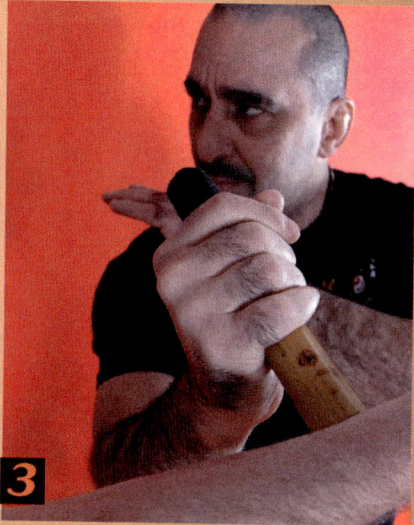

3

4

5

6

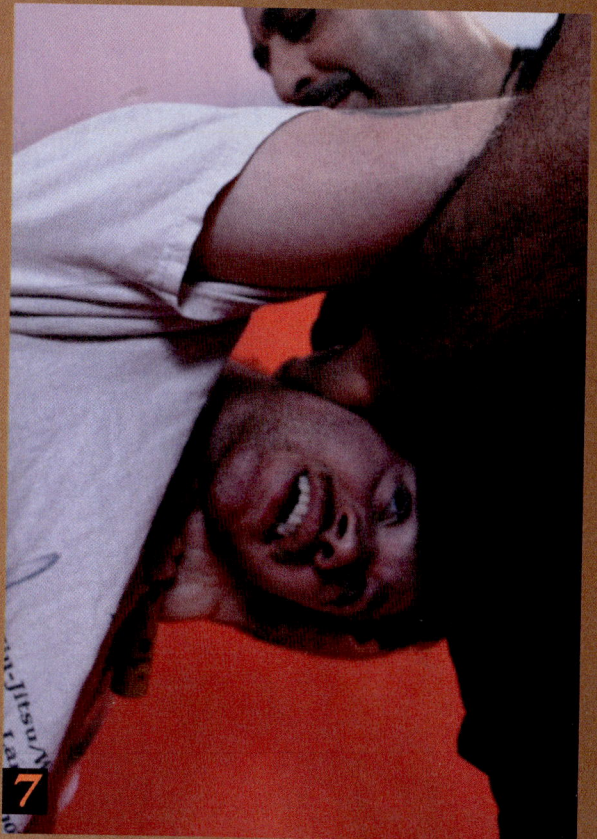

7

Martial Science
BIMONTHLY MAGAZINE OF MARTIAL ARTS   JUNE/2017 - N° 21
WWW.MARTIALSCIENCEMAGAZINE.COM

SHINE IN THE MUNICH HALL OF HONOURS 2017

SEIEIDO SELF DEFENSE
DAVE JOHNSON

NIHON JUJUTSU
GABRIEL GARCIA

SHINKAIDO RYU
HENRY BINERFA

ARUHONSO HA AIKIDO
SENSEI TONY JR

KENPO 5.0
THE PERFECT WEAPON
JEFF SPEAKMAN

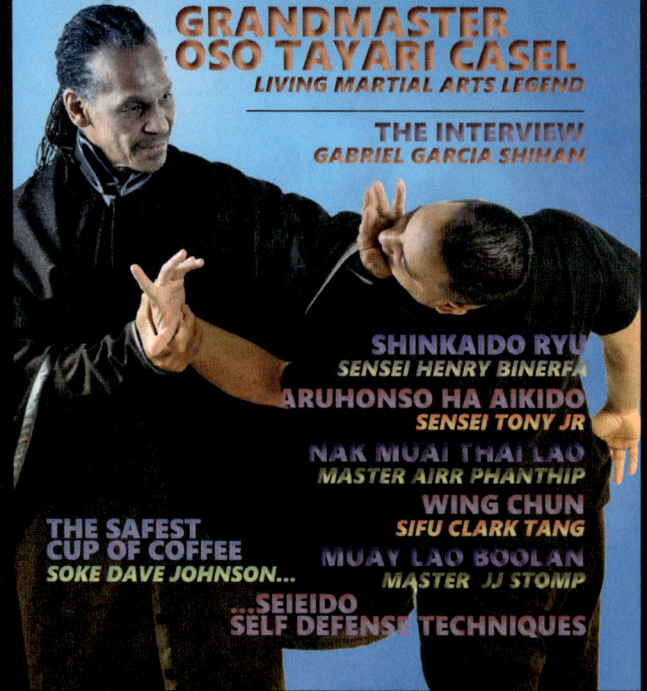

Martial Science
BIMONTHLY MAGAZINE OF MARTIAL ARTS   APRIL/2017 - N° 20
WWW.MARTIALSCIENCEMAGAZINE.COM

GRANDMASTER OSO TAYARI CASEL
LIVING MARTIAL ARTS LEGEND

THE INTERVIEW
GABRIEL GARCIA SHIHAN

SHINKAIDO RYU
SENSEI HENRY BINERFA

ARUHONSO HA AIKIDO
SENSEI TONY JR

NAK MUAI THAI LAO
MASTER AIRR PHANTHIP

WING CHUN
SIFU CLARK TANG

MUAY LAO BOOLAN
MASTER JJ STOMP

THE SAFEST CUP OF COFFEE
SOKE DAVE JOHNSON...

...SEIEIDO
SELF DEFENSE TECHNIQUES

Martial Science
BIMONTHLY MAGAZINE OF MARTIAL ARTS   AUGUST/2017 - N° 22
WWW.MARTIALSCIENCEMAGAZINE.COM

2017 MARTIAL ARTS SUPERSHOW

THE PROFESSOR:
TAI CHI'S JOURNEY WEST

JEFF SPEAKMAN TECHNIQUES

SHINKAIDO RYU TAMBO JUTSU
HENRY BINERFA

INTERVIEW MARK STAS WING FLOW SYSTEM
MASTER GUY EDWARD LARKE

KALI
INDIGENOUS ART OF THE PHILIPPINES
TUHON APOLO LADRA

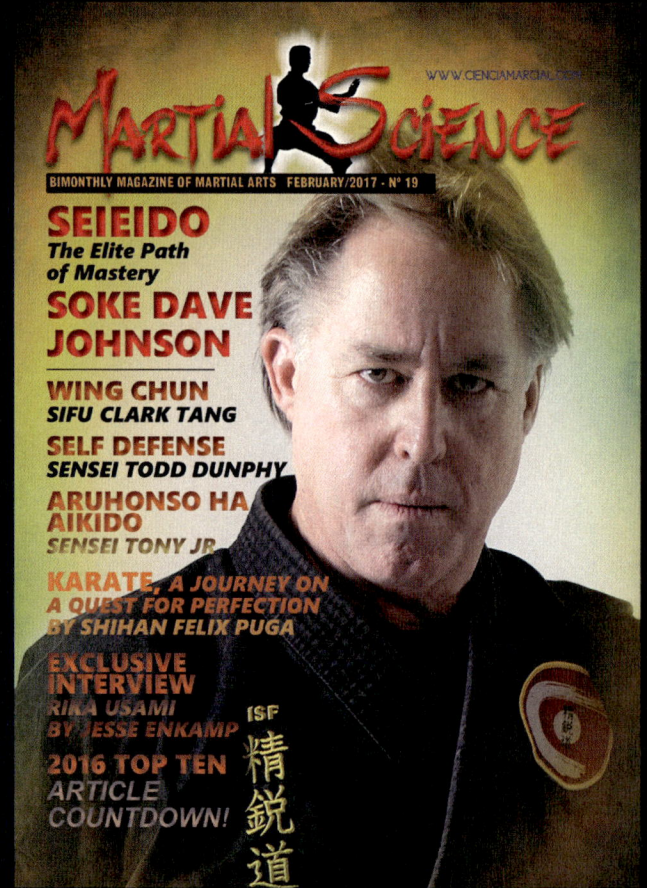

Martial Science
BIMONTHLY MAGAZINE OF MARTIAL ARTS   FEBRUARY/2017 - N° 19
WWW.CIENCIAMARTIAL.???

SEIEIDO
The Elite Path of Mastery
SOKE DAVE JOHNSON

WING CHUN
SIFU CLARK TANG

SELF DEFENSE
SENSEI TODD DUNPHY

ARUHONSO HA AIKIDO
SENSEI TONY JR

KARATE, A JOURNEY ON A QUEST FOR PERFECTION
BY SHIHAN FELIX PUGA

EXCLUSIVE INTERVIEW
RIKA USAMI BY JESSE ENKAMP

2016 TOP TEN ARTICLE COUNTDOWN!

ISF
精鋭道

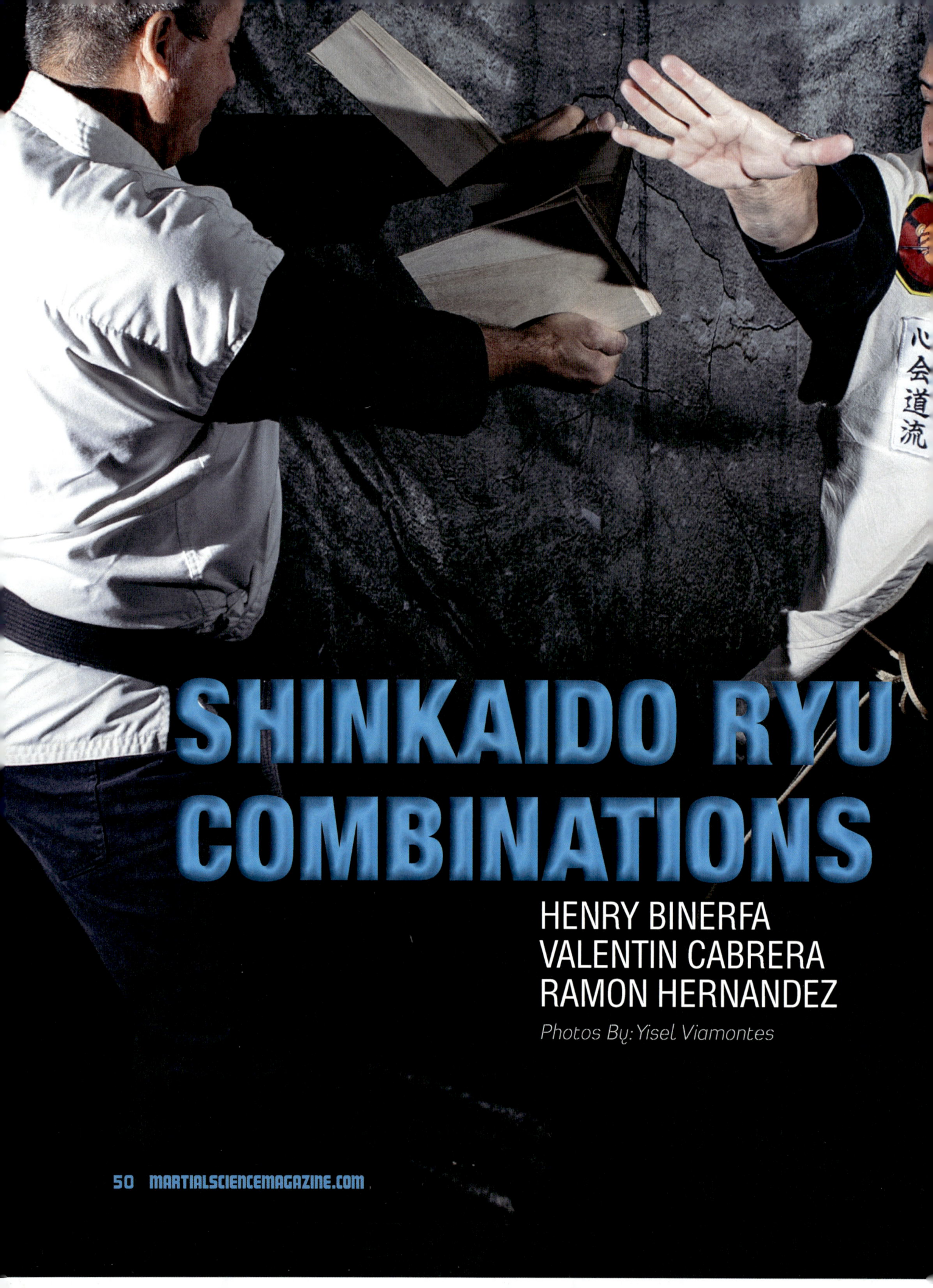

SHINKAIDO RYU COMBINATIONS

HENRY BINERFA
VALENTIN CABRERA
RAMON HERNANDEZ

Photos By: Yisel Viamontes

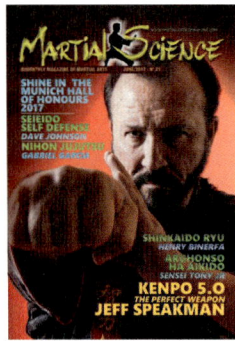

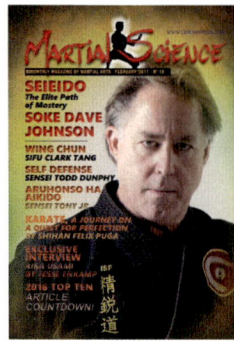

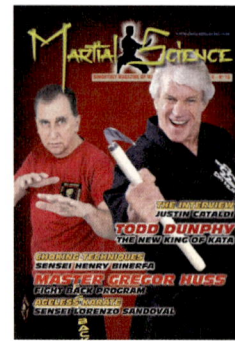

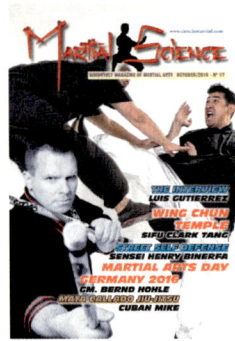

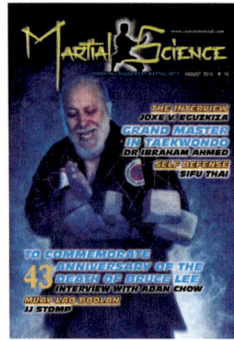

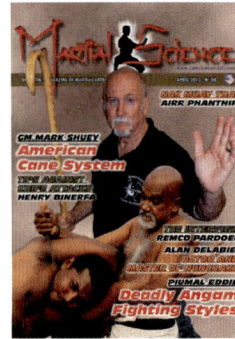

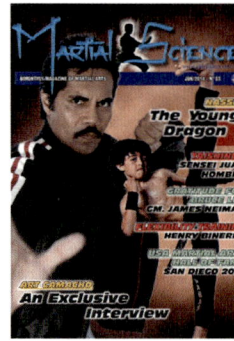

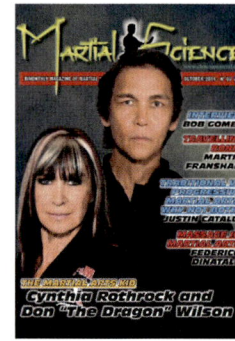

COMPLETE YOUR
COLLECTION, PURCHASE THE
BACK ISSUES OF

MARTIAL SCIENCE
MAGAZINE

Mitsuru Nagata was born in Kyoto in 1979 and started studying Shodou at the age 6. He has a degree in sociology from the Kyoto Buddhist University and for many years undertook several courses to perfect his technique but has developed his own personal and contemporary style that combines sumie and shodou. Japanese calligraphy or 'shodou' and 'sumie' are techniques of painting that are practiced in some Asian countries and are connected to Zen Buddhist philosophy and also require years of practice.

Mitsuru currently lives in Barcelona and participates in events, exhibitions and workshops to spread Japanese culture abroad. He has been a guest artist in several cities such as Barcelona, Madrid, Bilbao, Valencia, etc. where he has taught sumi-e and calligraphy classes, and he has done many live painting performances. He collaborates with the Japanese Embassy doing his live performances. Then he has worked for the creation of art for theater plays such as 'El tigre the yuzu'. He currently has an online store nagatayakyoto.net where he performs unique and personalized works of sumi-e and calligraphy and he also creates logos for brands.

nagatayakyoto.net

SELF DEFENSE PROGRAM
Master Gregor Huss

Photos By: Henry Binerfa

1

2

3

4

SELF DEFENSE

FIGHT BACK

PROGRAM

GREGOR HUSS

Made in the USA
Las Vegas, NV
23 January 2021